If you are feeling a little "l[...]" [...] Christmas this year, with all the [...] rounding the arrival of the January credit card bill, then I highly recommend this book to you. Readers beware . . . when you are finished, you will most definitely want to join the Advent Conspiracy movement. I did!

—**Randy Frazee**, pastor & author of many
books, including *Think, Act, Be Like Jesus*

Some books convey information, while others educate and also inspire. Only a few, however, spur a movement that reshapes culture. *Advent Conspiracy* is just such a book. It reframes our consumer-centered approach to Christmas into a Christ-centered calling. In so doing, it not only turns our energy outward into the kind of love Jesus came to model but sets us free to experience life and faith in the radical and transforming way God intends. This book will subversively change the way you look at Christmas and restore your life in the process.

—**Ken Wytsma**, lead pastor of Village
Church, Beaverton (Oregon) and
author of *The Myth of Equality*

The Advent Conspiracy has become a fully integrated part of our yearly rhythm and an effective way of directing our community's worship toward Jesus. If you are lamenting the dehumanizing culture of consumerism and are looking for true Joy, this book is a helpful tool for leading your congregation back to incarnation and compassion.

—**Door of Hope**

ADVENT CONSPIRACY

MAKING CHRISTMAS MEANINGFUL (AGAIN)

REVISED AND UPDATED

RICK MCKINLEY, CHRIS SEAY, GREG HOLDER

WITH CONTRIBUTIONS FROM CO-CONSPIRATORS AROUND THE WORLD

ZONDERVAN

Advent Conspiracy
Copyright © 2009, 2018 by Rick McKinley, Chris Seay, and Greg Holder

Requests for information should be addressed to:
Zondervan, 3900 *Sparks Dr. SE, Grand Rapids, Michigan* 49546

ISBN 978-0-310-35346-1 (softcover)

ISBN 978-0-310-35347-8 (ebook)

Published in association with Yates & Yates, www.yates2.com.

Cover design: Studio Gearbox
Cover illustrations: Olga Popova / ninocka / Shutterstock
Interior design: Denise Froehlich

First printing August 2018 / Printed in the United States of America

CONTENTS

THE MAKINGS OF A CONSPIRACY

FOUR THOUGHTS THAT COULD
STILL CHANGE THE WORLD

A LASTING LEGACY

THE MAKINGS OF A CONSPIRACY

INTRODUCTION

TEN YEARS LATER

I n some ways it is remarkable that a decade has come and gone since a handful of churches started dreaming of a different way to celebrate Christmas. But God has filled those ten-plus years with stories of meaning and worship.

And for this, we are grateful.

From the beginning this idea of a conspiracy made sense to us—we followers of King Jesus would *conspire* with other like-minded believers to resist what presses in on each of us during the Advent season. And for many, the idea of conspiring seemed just about right. For others, the word seemed a bit scary at first. Interviews we each gave to the media upon the initial release of the book would sometimes start with the name of this movement—and a question. "In a world of conspiracy theorists and so many who imagine one behind every tree, do we really need one more—you know—conspiracy?"

Of course, in some ways, this played out exactly as we had hoped. For yes, the world very much needed this kind of conspiracy, we would each explain. Together there was a better way, a fuller, richer way to celebrate the joy of the Christmas story. And this one not only protected our hearts (and in many cases, our budgets), but it offered protection and care for those in our world who are most exposed—*the least of these*, as Jesus so lovingly referred to them. It seemed like a win-win.

Well, not to everyone.

There were those who questioned our patriotism when we began to call for spending less. At that particular time, some would suggest we could spend our way out of the economic doldrums in which our country was then mired. "Don't you want things to improve?" one national commentator asked on a widely watched network. And then there was a rather famous and long-standing member of the television show *The View* who most decidedly did not agree with our tenets or our intent.

But then there were the others.

Our first year, the three churches we lead invested some capital in this movement to help get the word out: a website and a video explaining what we were up to. Who knew that day in December it would be the most viewed video on YouTube?

It seemed we weren't alone in thinking there must be a better way to celebrate the glorious story of Jesus' birth. Over the course of the next years, this conspiracy began to resonate with people around the world, each employing their own expressions of the four tenets that you will soon discover. Today, thousands of churches and various groups have conspired with us.

Because of the nature of the Advent Conspiracy and the fact that no money is given to us, it is impossible to know completely just how much money has been given to others—in local communities and to global organizations—all in the name of Jesus. But as you'll see, the stories reveal that something has indeed happened. When local churches agree to partner together to address an issue close to home, something is happening. When children begin to explain to their reliably generous grandparents that they only want one gift, and they'd like the rest of the money that their grandparents planned to spend to be used to help children halfway around the world, something is happening. When successful business owners on their early steps toward Jesus give for the first time to a Christian organization at Christmas, something is happening. When senior adults find purpose and a sense that they can still make a difference, when the very young start thinking entrepreneurally for the sake of the kingdom, something is happening.

When people in developing countries—many of whom could be on the receiving end of all this giving—ask if they too can participate in this conspiracy by giving to those even less fortunate, something is happening that could only be born in the mind of God himself. This was truly the body of Christ working together for the sake of his kingdom and the good of our world. When other countries took these tenets and translated them to their own culture (for example, the much cooler sounding *Les Rebelles de Noel* of France), what was happening was now completely and forever out of our control. Not that it ever was ours to control.

But over the years in some very obvious ways, this call to a different way of celebrating Christmas became a Spirit-led revolution. And we believe God is just getting started. In fact, it is now time for us to pray for the same Spirit of God to breathe new life into this dream. It has been a fun ride, but now is the time for each of us to invite others into this grand plan of our good God. May conspirators young and old; rich and not-so-rich; in churches large and small, urban, suburban, and rural vow never to go back to the old, exhausting ways. May God remind us in obvious and not-so-obvious ways that the worship of his Son this Advent can still spark a revolution the likes of which the world hasn't seen.

CHAPTER 1

A RADICAL IDEA

THE BEGINNING OF A MOVEMENT

Imagine: The creator of the cosmos chose, from among his numberless galaxies and spinning stars, one tiny rock of a planet on which he entered human life in the most natural and self-effacing of ways—through the womb of a willing teenage girl.

His was one of many births that night, no doubt, but it was unique: God became a wailing, wrinkled newborn birthed onto the bloody straw of life on our sin-sick planet.

Perhaps only the angels knew what they were really witnessing. Their voices rang through the heavens, singing, "Glory to God in the highest!" Glory to God for the gift of his Son; glory to God for the cosmos-dwarfing love that led to the birth of a King in a rough stable.

There is a sense of prophetic mystery surrounding Christ's birth. The story reveals something divine to us; it drives our quest to look closely at our own stories. *Who are we? Why are we? How do we? Where, in the midst of our questions, is this Immanuel, this God-with-us?*

MISSING OUT

Sadly, for all our questioning, the mystery of the Incarnation still escapes us. Jesus comes, in his first Advent, into the midst of our great sin and suffering. This was God's design. But apart from the angels nudging a few scared shepherds and a cryptic star decoded by a handful of distant astrologists, almost everyone else simply missed it.

Are we any different?

Each year many of us routinely miss the wonder of God's miraculous birth. Reading those words even now should fill us with awe. But our overstuffed Decembers leave us wanting more. Our hyperconsumption leaves us empty. We worship less. We spend more. We give less. We struggle more.

Less, more. More, less. Time and nerves stretch thin, and we reduce family and friends to a card or a present that costs the "right" amount to prove our level of love. Our quest to celebrate mystery exhausts us. Another Christmas has passed by like a blizzard, and we are left to shovel through the trash of our failure.

This can't be right.

Missing the prophetic mystery of Jesus' birth means

missing God-with-us, God beside us—God becoming one of us. Missing out on Jesus changes everything.

BACK TO THE STABLE

Several years ago, a few of us were lamenting how we'd come to the end of an Advent season exhausted and sensing we'd missed it again: the awe-inducing, soul-satisfying mystery of the Incarnation. No wonder there was a dread at the beginning of each new season as we prepared to proclaim, celebrate, and worship around the story of God entering our world as one of us. Something was just not right. A creeping kind of idolatry was consuming us along with our congregations.

We were drowning in a sea of financial debt and endless lists of gifts to buy. We had believed the marketing lie that the spending of money is the best way to express love and, in true American fashion, "more must be better." (Such a tale is still convincing enough to make "believers" out of non-Christians and Christians alike.)

It was in that moment of brutal honesty that we admitted our fear: on Christmas Day, God would come near—as he always does and always is—and we would miss it yet again.

So we decided to try an experiment: What if, instead of acting like bystanders to the nativity, we led our congregations *into* the nativity story as participants?

We didn't know what to expect, but we knew we needed to reclaim the story of Christmas, the foundational narrative of the church. As we strove to see the birth of Christ from inside the stable instead of inside the mall, our holiday practices began to change.

SPEND LESS. GIVE MORE. WORSHIP MORE.

If it doesn't take money to love, a recalculation is needed. If love is to be the driving force of our gift giving, then money cannot be. Our dominating culture of consumerism can, and must, be rejected. When we refuse to equate money with love, we become free. Free to leave the shallow story of cultural Christmas and enter the deep, life-giving waters of the Incarnation. Free to give without comparison, receive with gratitude, and worship with abandon.

Children understand the creative joy of making gifts, the excitement of giving themselves away. Watching our own children, and receiving their love, we remembered that we didn't need a price tag to quantify our love. Spending less freed us to give more. We replaced material *presents* with the gift of *presence.* We learned to give our time, our talents, our love, and ourselves to one another.

Since the inception of the Conspiracy, the entire Christmas offering that is collected during our multiple Christmas Eve services leaves our midst—no matter how much is given or where we are with the budget. This public commitment to worship Jesus by giving to the "least of these" has changed us and, with God's help, the world.

We were convinced that an inescapable consequence of truly entering the Christmas story was a compulsion to love all. We were reminded of Jesus' teaching, that whenever we see a brother or sister hungry or cold, whatever we do to the least of these, so we do to him. To love Jesus, we needed to love and serve the outcast, poor, and ignored among us—in our local schools, in faraway villages, and under highway overpasses as the mechanisms of progress speed by.

Spending less gave us the resources to make a huge difference—and the greatest resource was the presence of Christ within us. With our new freedom of time-space and mind-space, our attention was more ably focused on Jesus' coming. For the first time in many years, we felt as if we were on our knees in the dirt beside the manger, worshiping with the shepherds. Jesus was being experienced among us in living, transforming, beautiful, and fresh ways, and the stories of changed lives multiplied greater than we could ever imagine. Nothing seemed impossible for God . . . and it didn't stop at Christmas.

DREAMING BIGGER DREAMS

When we considered that the coming of Christ was good news for all people, we began to realize that meant everyone. Not just our friends and neighbors but *everyone*. All people for all time. So we began to think of how this announcement could show up in tangible ways all over the world. One of our friends began to be burdened about the world water crisis.

The water crisis around the world is staggering. Hundreds of children die simply because they don't have access to clean drinking water. It makes our mouths drop and our stomachs turn when we realize that the amount of money we spend on Christmas in America is close to forty-five times the amount of money it would take to supply the entire world with clean water. What if some of the money we spent at Christmas was used to dig wells for poor or remote communities in which people die regularly from the lack of clean water? Partnering with Living Water International, we began dreaming of using the money we saved from worshiping more and spending less and were able to build many wells.

We will never forget receiving the email telling us that the water crisis in Mount Barclay, Liberia, was solved! Children splashing the fresh water and praising God simply because people on the other side of the world began to be more faithful to the message of Christmas. That's simply one way the message went out.

Over the last few years, we traveled at Christmas to these villages with new wells to celebrate the hope of Jesus with them. Imagine children dancing and shouting as clean water gushes into the air. Picture people worshiping Jesus with glass after glass: "Living water for our souls, clean water for our bodies." Consider that each well was drilled with money that was rightly given as a birthday gift to Jesus himself.

It wasn't just wells either; there were tangible local expressions that the announcement of Christ was good news to the least of these in our own communities. One church threw open the doors at the local school so 150 of the poorest families in their community could come and receive clothing, food, and some simple gifts for their kids. People hung out and wrapped presents and played with kids so the parents could shop. As one person described it: "We felt it in the air that Christmas really can still change the world."

Believing that, we dreamed even bigger: What if we invited more faith communities to join us? We put together a few thousand dollars, launched a website, and invited others to join the Advent Conspiracy Jesus began so many years ago on a night in Bethlehem.

The story caught on, and people joined us. Hundreds upon hundreds of churches began to worship fully, spend less, give more, and love all. It became a movement that is still growing today. Churches all over the world are joining the Advent Conspiracy and discovering Jesus in a way that is changing lives. Entering the story was harder than we thought, more meaningful than we dared to dream, and one of the most beautiful encounters with Jesus that many of us have ever experienced.

Now tens of thousands of people all over the world are meeting the King born in a stable and serving his beloved, needy children. This book is about the radical idea that we can celebrate the Advent of Jesus Christ humbly, beautifully, and generously. It has always been our dream that every Jesus follower would worship fully, spend less, give more, and courageously love all in the name and power of Jesus.

In some ways it is common sense. But in other ways it will still seem radically different. To see it become a reality, we had to (and must still) conspire together to make it happen.

So we refuse to be defined by our culture. Instead, emboldened by the Spirit, we are now re-creating culture in the name of the good, the true, and the beautiful Jesus Christ.

A STORY, NOT A SYSTEM

The Advent Conspiracy is not a four-point checklist for how to do Christmas. It is not a formula or a foolproof system to make your Christmas more meaningful.

The Advent Conspiracy is the story of the wondrous moment when God entered our world to make things right. It is the greatest story ever told, and it changes everything—including the way we celebrate Christmas.

As you read this book, understand what you're doing and why you're doing it. This is not about anger, disgust, or guilt about how Christmas has been co-opted. It is about entering the story of Jesus more deeply with a desire to worship more fully. It is not enough to say no to the way Christmas is celebrated by many; we need to say yes to a different way of celebrating.

A newlywed couple started the tradition of buying tickets to the symphony for Christmas. They invite their family, and together they get dressed up, have dinner, and go to the concert. Each Christmas the whole family looks forward to this special night.

Our hope is that as you read this book you will discover Christ and be transformed by entering his story. The idea is simple, yet sometimes it is simple ideas that change our lives in the best way possible.

The message of Jesus can still change the world. We continue to conspire together and discover new and creative ways in which Jesus can liberate the world. Will you write your life into his story? Will you consider this radical idea?

CHAPTER 2

IDOLATRY NEAR THE MANGER

ALTARS TO THE WRONG GOD

E very day advertisements implore us to get more from life. Fulfillment is within our grasp—and we deserve it. Why wait when we can have everything now?

We can buy the house of our dreams with no money down. We can pull a fine bottle of French wine from our miniature wine cellar and savor the flavors while we sit on our suede sectional and watch the smartest, flattest TV on the market. Before going to sleep on our third new mattress in five years, we go online to pay our bills and then mindlessly order a few more Christmas presents—and something for ourselves so we can get free shipping.

We have been told that this is the perfect life. We assume that when we get to this point, we will be satisfied. Yet if we spend our lives pursuing this dream, we discover that it cannot deliver on its grand promises of ease and satisfaction. These things do not satisfy; there will always be a better phone, a cooler car, a faster computer; the latest and greatest is soon tomorrow's old news. We end up running a race for something that never ends, feeling more alone and less satisfied with every lap.

A FAST-GROWING RELIGION

The fastest growing religion in the world is not Islam or Christianity; the symbol of this rising faith is not the star and crescent or the cross but a dollar sign. This expanding belief system is radical consumerism. It promises transcendence, power, pleasure, and fulfillment even as it demands complete devotion.

Many Christians have decided they can, to put it bluntly, love both God and money. Our Scriptures tell how God's people were often intrigued by the promises of other gods, whether offering a bountiful harvest, sexual pleasure, or political power. God's people did not denounce God as they began to worship Baal or any other false god. Rather, they often continued to profess loyalty to God while they pursued their functional god. In the same way, Christians have incorporated their devotion to consumerism with their Christian faith. With every decision comes a quiet compromise. Stone by stone, our monument to another god grows.

It is now clear that a primary threat to true Christianity in America is consumerism—not liberalism, fundamentalism, Darwinism, secularism, or any other -ism that happens to achieve some level of influence and power.

Consumerism promises transcendence. Our consumer culture claims that the material thing we want most will elevate us above our current circumstances. A car, for example, is not simply a form of transportation: a car offers status, mystique, thrills, adventure, and confidence. If it were otherwise, we would all be driving the simplest, most cost-effective car available. Yet we buy cars for more than function, wondering which model will be the best for us. These promises are not completely empty—for weeks or months we may wake up happier knowing that we will be driving the car of our dreams. Inside, however, we know this sort of happiness is fleeting, whether it ends in a crash or the slow creep of longing for an even better car.

A family agreed not to exchange presents but instead gave that money to a charity or cause of their own choosing. On Christmas Day, the time around the tree was spent listening as each person described their gift and why that cause mattered to them.

The same is true of small purchases. Clothes protect our bodies from the weather and fit social norms. Yet most of us buy clothes to help us feel more attractive and successful. How many of us have ever put on a new outfit for a date or a fashionable suit for an interview?

In the religion of consumerism, the thing we desire becomes the symbol of whatever meaning it insinuates. Because we buy into the meaning, we believe we have become more significant, able to rise above the circumstances, frustrations, and mundane moments of our everyday lives. In short, our consumerism tells us that we'll be reborn.

Yet all too soon the luster starts to fade. We tell ourselves not to worry because there's another package to open, another order to place, or another website to scroll through. Another messiah has come into our consumer world to save us from our self-created agony.

YOUR DISSATISFACTION IS GUARANTEED

Consumerism demands that we be dissatisfied. You will never hear a salesman say, "Great news! This is the last one of these you'll ever need to buy." We are constantly searching for the one thing that will satisfy us.

Yet each time we trust the promises of our possessions, more barriers are raised between our true selves and God's plain command to love him above all things. It's not that we necessarily want more—it's that what we want is something we can't buy.

Consumerism can also poison our relationship with Christ. Jesus becomes a commodity we consume rather than a King who reigns. We tried Jesus. We were satisfied for six months, but then something about him just didn't meet our needs, and now we're ready to trade him in like a leased car for something better. Because we've been so deeply formed by a culture of consumerism, we cannot fathom the lasting value of Jesus.

Besides making false promises, this mind-set of overconsumption detaches us from the human cost of the products we buy. Most of the time we have no idea how our shirt was made, who made it, or where it came from. It's practically magic: we can spend a few dollars and a new product travels across the world to our waiting arms.

Now imagine picking out a shirt and hanging with the tag is a picture of the Guatemalan woman who earned thirty-three cents an hour sewing that shirt. There is no way any corporation is going to show us that picture because we might start calculating: "Wait . . .

thirty-three cents an hour, twelve hours a day, six days a week . . . and they want forty bucks for the shirt?"

No, this will require that our consciences stay detached from the moral consequences of our purchases. We buy without thinking beyond the price and the false promise of a newer, better self. Yet we ought not to deceive ourselves: this has the makings of a religion centered around us, and thus it becomes a form of worship.

Sometimes uncovering the truth seems so overwhelming that we wonder if it's even worth the effort. To speak bluntly of other gods is an uncomfortable thing. It is much easier to keep playing the game and pretending all is well. Meanwhile, this other altar is built, costing us more than we can ever imagine. It's much easier to bow down once again before the god of consumerism, to assume there's nothing we can do to make anything better. We keep playing the game and pretending everything is okay.

But is it?

This lesser god is a snarling monster with razor-sharp teeth. It devours not only those from whom it takes but also those who eagerly receive its plunder. James (the brother of Jesus) warns us of these dangers, saying:

Hey, you rich folk, misery is on its way; so cry and moan because you will watch your riches rot before your eyes as the moths devour your fine clothes. Your stockpile of silver and gold is tarnished and corroded, and this rust will stand up in the final judgment and testify against you. It will eat your flesh like fire and become a permanent and painful reminder that you have hoarded your wealth through these last days. Listen. You held back a just wage from the laborers who mowed your fields, and that money is crying out against you, demanding that justice be done.[1]

Left unchecked, our constant pursuit of the next big thing has fatal consequences. Our hyperconsumption all too easily becomes plundering and pillaging. "You'd better be on your guard," Jesus warned, "against any type of greed, for a person's life is not about having a lot of possessions."[2] Despite this caution, many of us still seem eager to give it a try.

LESS IS MORE

By definition, Christians believe that the most important gifts in the world are not the things we can see and touch. So what happens when we single-mindedly pursue material wealth? When we think of trouble, we tend to picture hardships and disease and accidents and domestic turmoil. Images of poverty and squalor and wretchedness may come to mind. Yet the real trouble we often face wears a very different mask.

A large urban church decided that part of their Advent giving would be focused on local efforts. After realizing the significant need in their city, they partnered with another local church and helped fund a new church building in an underserved area.

In ancient times, God led the Israelites out of slavery, a brutal captivity in which their children had been euthanized, their work had been almost physically impossible, and they lacked basic religious freedom. God intimidated their captors with terrifying plagues, parted the Red Sea to make possible their escape, and led them by pillars of cloud and fire to a good land he had promised them. On their journey to freedom, water burst from the rocks and manna rained daily from the sky.

How did the people respond to this remarkable provision? They complained: "We want meat!" "We're sick of this funky bread!" God, in his infinite wisdom, gave these ungrateful, murmuring people exactly what they asked for. "I'll give you meat," he said, "and you will eat it. Not for one day, ten days, or twenty—you will eat it until you vomit it out your nostrils."[3] Trouble in the form of *plenty*? You bet.

In these days it seems God has done the same for the West: "You want wealth above all else? I will give you more than any other society has ever enjoyed—and it will lead to your destruction." The founder of Frontier Mission Fellowship, Ralph Winter, writes: "The underdeveloped societies suffer from one set of diseases: tuberculosis, malnutrition, pneumonia, parasites, typhoid, cholera, typhus, etc. Affluent America has virtually invented a whole new set of diseases: obesity, arteriosclerosis, heart disease, stroke, lung cancer, venereal disease, cirrhosis of the liver, drug addiction, alcoholism . . . In saving ourselves we have nearly lost ourselves."[4]

When "more" becomes our highest aim, the greatest danger comes when we get exactly what we want—more. More debt, more struggle, more dissatisfaction, more envy, more . . . well, you get the idea.

What if, instead of pursuing the latest gadgets and most comfortable of lifestyles, we became pilgrims like the Magi? What if we left behind our ease in order to witness—and worship—something (or someone) infinitely better?

In our hearts we know that mindless consuming is not the Christian way to celebrate the birth of Christ. Could opting out of the cultural traps set throughout the Christmas season give us the chance to worship truly and love all? Might it be that the King of Kings is more powerful, and more worthy of our trust, than any lesser god? What might happen as we humbly set out to dismantle this altar to a false god? Are we really willing to spend less and receive more?

FOUR THOUGHTS THAT COULD STILL CHANGE THE WORLD

CHAPTER 3

WORSHIP FULLY

THE MISSING INGREDIENT

Our hearts are formed by what we worship. Excitement, anticipation, hope—each of these emotions swells around the object of our dearest affection. We spend our time and energy on what matters most to us.

What do we worship during Advent? "Jesus" is the right answer, of course, but is it the true answer? Does the way we spend our time, money, and energy testify that we worship God incarnate? Season after season, many churchgoers have learned to say the right things without allowing their words to reach their hearts. Simply saying that Jesus is the desire of our hearts doesn't make it so. In fact, proper, expected words can sometimes hinder true worship by keeping our lips and hearts apart.

Looking honestly at the desires of our hearts is scarier than simply saying what people expect or demand. Kids don't suffer from this fear. Ask a child what she is excited about at Christmas, and it's doubtful she'll exclaim with passion, "Jesus' birthday!" Before she's been indoctrinated with the proper religious mantra, she'll tell you about that shiny blue bike that she can't *wait* to ride on Christmas morning.

The things we desire are the things we worship. During Advent—a time of conspicuous consumption—we need to look closely at what we want and desire. Let's think beyond the well-rehearsed responses and strive to discover what is really in our hearts.

We spend hundreds of billions of dollars during the holiday season, hoping—whether we admit it to ourselves or not—that the latest and greatest gift will fulfill us and those we give gifts to. This (we think) will bring us joy. This will make our Christmas memorable. We sprint through store after store or, these days, scroll through page after page on Amazon, trying to find the perfect gift to express our love because we crave to be loved in return. We long for peace in place of the annual holiday family soap opera. We shop till we drop so we can finally rest. We go into debt and assume we're entitled to whatever we want.

We sit in church drained and exhausted—but still restless because we're too far from the stable to see much of anything.

The heart of what we're truly searching for—hope, peace, love, rest, worship—is buried in the seasonal chaos. Each step we take toward an overstuffed schedule and an overextended budget is one step further away from the nativity.

ENTER CHRISTMAS

The time of year when focusing on Christ should be the easiest is often the hardest. The invitation to join the Advent Conspiracy is a call to remain at the side of the baby Jesus and worship him—no matter how strongly the cultural demands of Christmas pull at us. The transformation initiated by Jesus is no different today than it was the day he was born—the source of joy, peace, and hope hasn't changed.

What if we could enter the story of Christ's coming in a fresh way? Read this father's account of how his young son began to experience the birth of Jesus in a service at Ecclesia:

My family had been talking about the birth of Christ and what it meant that God gave himself to be with us. I could see my children processing, but I didn't know if it was really connecting. But during an Advent worship service, my son brought his allowance savings without telling me. As our sanctuary filled with voices celebrating the birth of Christ, we went forward to the communion table. Looking down at my son, I saw him put something like $40 into the offering for kids around the world. When I asked him about it later, he said he wanted to give like God had given to us.

Each year Advent brings another opportunity to worship the miracle of the Incarnation when God revealed himself to people in a new way. Nearly every character who encounters the infant King in the Advent story has the same response: worship. Their worship sprang from deep places of the heart that were touched for the first time by God-in-the-flesh. Such worship challenges old beliefs about God and what it means to be present with him.

THE INVITATION: MARY

Mary was a teenage girl engaged to marry a poor carpenter named Joseph. She lived on a dusty fringe of the mighty Roman Empire, just another powerless peasant in another backwater town. Yet she was the woman to whom God extended the invitation to be the mother of the Messiah Jesus.

In Luke's account, Gabriel, God's archangel, announces to Mary that she has found favor with God—she will give birth to a child, and she will name him Jesus. Mary's response—"Here I am, the Lord's humble servant. As you have said, let it be done to me"[1]—is as simple as it is inspiring. She doesn't protest or let her fear sway her from following God.

Mary joins the rich tradition of Jewish poets and prophets as she composes a song of devotion to her Lord:

> My soul lifts up the Lord!
> My spirit celebrates God, my Liberator!
> For though I'm God's humble servant,
> God has noticed me.
> Now and forever,
> I will be considered blessed by all generations.
> For the Mighty One has done great things for me;
> holy is God's name!
> From generation to generation,
> God's lovingkindness endures
> for those who revere Him.
> God's arm has accomplished mighty deeds.

> The proud in mind and heart,
>
> God has sent away in disarray.
>
> The rulers from their high positions of power,
>
> God has brought down low.
>
> And those who were humble and lowly,
>
> God has elevated with dignity.
>
> The hungry—God has filled with fine food.
>
> The rich—God has dismissed with nothing in
>
> their hands.
>
> To Israel, God's servant,
>
> God has given help,
>
> As promised to our ancestors,
>
> remembering Abraham and his
>
> descendants in mercy forever.[2]

Mary's song is known as the Magnificat because she magnifies God, pointing to him as she worships and confesses his great love for and future deliverance of the oppressed.

We are not the humble lifted by God of whom Mary sings. We are the powerful, the rich, the self-absorbed. Hundreds of millions of people throughout the world live without clean water, housing, food, and education. These are the humble and hungry to whom Mary promises deliverance. Through her son, the

Messiah, tyrants will be defeated and the oppressed will be liberated and ushered into a kingdom that will have no end.

Mary announces that God is here! She carries him in her womb. The mystery of the moment is mind-bending. This Liberating King is nothing less than her son and her God. Mary's worship begins with the ultimate paradox: a young girl, unwed and without power, influence, or wealth, cradles within her womb the divine power of the universe. The Creator who spoke creation into place is taking on fingers and toes inside her belly, and the One who holds all wealth of the universe will soon nurse at her breast. Jesus is a fetus inside the worshiping Mary, who recognizes through grace that this great God is doing a great thing for all people!

How can we join Mary's Magnificat? Is the warm feeling we get when we sing "Silent Night" fitting worship for our King? Of course. But perhaps Advent can elicit even more than warm emotions. What do we owe a God who entered our world to bring justice to his children? With Mary as our model, let poets pen odes, musicians compose songs, and prophets stand and call us to see what God sees: the birth of his Son signifies the beginning of the end of injustice.

A young woman started her AC journey by sponsoring a goat and a water well through World Vision in her in-laws' names. The following year, the rest of the family joined in. She said, "I love that I can impact someone halfway around the world and at the same time de-stress my own holiday season."

Let our worship be an outpouring of our hearts. Let us take God's self-revelation seriously as we begin to desire the same things that move his perfect heart. Let our worship drive us from the enclosure of church walls and out into painful places that cry out for God's liberation. Author Mark Labberton puts it this way:

This disparity between economics and justice is an issue of worship. According to the narrative of Scripture, the very heart of how we show and distinguish true worship from false worship is apparent in how we respond to the poor, the oppressed, the neglected, and the forgotten. As of now, I do not see this theme troubling the waters of worship in the American church. But justice and mercy are not add-ons to worship, nor are they the consequences of worship. Jesus and mercy are intrinsic to God and therefore intrinsic to the worship of God.[3]

THE GIFT OF HOSPITALITY: ELIZABETH

When young Mary needed a safe place where she could escape the harsh stares and gossipy whispers of her small village, she visited some relatives out of town. Making the journey from Nazareth to a town in the hill country of Judea, Mary found her cousin Elizabeth living with her own miracle pregnancy. Much older and apparently past the expected age of bearing children, she was about to give birth to one of Israel's most colorful prophets (and that's saying something). In the coming years he would be known as John the Baptizer, the one who prepared the way for Mary's baby—Israel's Messiah.

But before either of these little boys was born, two women shared their stories of God's incredible power.

How desperately Mary must've longed for at least someone—*anyone*—to believe her tale of an angelic visitor and a once-in-forever pregnancy. It was in the home of Elizabeth (and Zechariah, her temporarily muted husband) that she found what she needed. In the coming days and years, Mary would no doubt encounter many who doubted her story (and her son) and more than a few who came to believe every glorious detail. But it was the warm hospitality during that first Advent that soothed Mary's soul.

Elizabeth provided a safe and loving refuge for her cousin, who was questioned and possibly rejected by everyone else. In what tangible ways can we "practice hospitality" as Paul tells us in Romans 12? Are there specific people this Christmas we can invite into our midst? Is it possible that all these years later, one of the ways we can still celebrate Advent is by honoring those who never thought they'd be welcomed by anyone?

At The Crossing, there is a private dinner each December for women who've left the sex trade. It is sponsored and held by other women in the church who champion these courageous steps that are taken all year long. But at Advent, women from various backgrounds gather at a table to consider again the birth of Jesus and what it might still mean for each of them. There are no insiders or outsiders at this meal, only sisters who will laugh and cry and pray and remember that Jesus is indeed the King who came to liberate each of us.

What might this look like for you? With whom can you share a meal? Who in your midst could never imagine or dare hope that they might be invited to the table? If the ancient practice of hospitality showed up in the Christmas story, why can't it show up in our Advent season? What might happen if you did "take every opportunity to open your life and home to others?"[4]

A HOLY DRAMA: JOSEPH

Joseph, the earthly father of Jesus, goes from model citizen to soap opera star overnight. His fiancée is pregnant, and the baby isn't his. In Joseph's world, this was beyond taboo. Though Joseph could have exposed Mary to public shame and punishment, he decides to discreetly break off the engagement and let things end as quietly as possible.

That's when the angel shows up. In a dream, God's messenger tells Joseph not to break his pledge to Mary because her baby was conceived by the Holy Spirit. He will be called Jesus, meaning our "salvation" or "God's rescue." Matthew's Gospel points to the book of Isaiah as a resource: "A virgin will conceive and bear a Son, and His name will be Immanuel (which is a Hebrew name that means 'God with us')."[5]

God came in person to walk with us as one of us.

God is saving the world because he entered into the very situation he wants to heal.

When we worship Jesus at Christmas, we're reminded that God came for all humanity. No matter our momentary circumstances, every human needs to be rescued from sin by the sacred Son. We in the West, in particular, need to be rescued from our own self-centered agendas, from our ability to become bored with "God with us," Immanuel.

Joseph chose obedience. However scared he was of what his mother would say or his friends would think, he still took Mary home to be his wife. He was a fool—a holy fool who gave up his reputation and rights because of a call from God.

One of the common fears people have about the Advent Conspiracy is what their relatives might think, do, feel, or say. Quite honestly, in this day and time, it does sound crazy at first to spend less, to give more, and to use our holiday money to love our brothers and sisters around the world. Joseph, however, reminds us that while the call of God isn't always easy or conventional, it is always right—and God will give us the courage to follow if we are willing to obey. Like Joseph, when we act in obedience to God's invitation—despite even the social cost—we help God's will be done on earth as it is in heaven.

RESPONDING TO THE CALL: THE SHEPHERDS

Another of God's angelic messengers brought the news of Jesus' birth to shepherds working nearby. At that time, shepherds were often despised as thieves unfit for more respectable occupations. Their testimony was not allowed in court nor their presence in polite society, so shepherds found their place on the outskirts of towns. Often young, aged, or female, they were largely shunned by the mainstream population.

Yet we are loved by a God who sees the overlooked. He looks at our hearts, not our place in society. So at the birth of his only Son, God chose a group of people, invisible to most of the world, to celebrate the good news of their Savior's birth. After hearing from God, the shepherds immediately went to witness the miracle for themselves, after which they spread the glorious news far and wide.

Are we willing to respond to this call to leave our responsibilities and hurry off to see this miracle? To pause long enough to look upon the Savior who is Christ the Lord? Will we miss the invitation?

Long after the angels left, the shepherds continued to worship. Communities that have joined the Advent

Conspiracy have had similar experiences. We may not have seen the angelic host that awed the shepherds, but we are experiencing a sustainable worship that transcends the season of Christmas. The good news of the birth of Jesus moves into a world that needs him in every season.

A couple from Imago Dei Community in Portland reimagined their wedding in light of the Advent story:

> We participated in Advent Conspiracy for two years, and we deeply believed in the value of celebrating the Advent season by worshiping Christ through relational activity and giving our time and resources to those in need. When it came time to plan our wedding day, we realized the wedding industry was commercialized much like Christmas—the average American wedding costs $27,000! We asked ourselves, "Does celebrating our marriage require us to accrue large amounts of debt, or would God desire the emphasis to be placed elsewhere?"
>
> The answer we came to was the same answer we discovered through entering the story of Advent: God desires this to be a fundamentally *relational* event rather than a *consumer* event. Pursuing our own "Covenant Conspiracy," we chose to build the

wedding around worshiping God and celebrating our relationships with friends and family. We intentionally limited the amount of money we spent. We asked our guests to take the money they would have spent on wedding gifts, and give that money to Living Water International. Over $2,500 was given to help build wells around the world, while the entire wedding and reception cost less than $2,000.

Just as we experienced Christ during Advent, we found great joy in celebrating relationships and giving to "the least of these"—a greater joy by far than if we had simply followed the story our culture is telling us.

Living out our worship in tangible ways begins here and becomes the way we are invited to live and breathe in the moments of the glorious ordinary of our lives.

FROM A GREAT DISTANCE: THE WISE MEN

The Magi were scholars and astrologers from Persia and Babylon, east of Judea. After noticing a change in the star patterns in the sky, they began the long and arduous journey to Jerusalem, looking for the one the ancient texts foretold would be born King of the Jews.

The reigning king was Herod the Great. Although not a Jewish king, he had gained power through political marriages and carefully cultivated friendships with influential Romans. Herod protected his empire—in a backwater corner of the Roman Empire—with military might, bribery, and violent acts that extended even to members of his own family.

The Magi must have been people of some influence because they were given an audience with the king. They had the courage to ask Herod for directions to where the one true King was born so they could worship him. (Here's where most of us can find our inclusion becoming evident in God's redemptive story, since these men who were not even Jewish were willing to risk their lives to answer the call of the newborn King.)

Our Liberating King's entrance stands in contrast with Herod's tyranny—and that of the surrounding empires. Herod's citizens were controlled by military power, financial strength, and technological development. But Jesus' kingdom rises up differently. Jesus reveals his kingdom in vulnerability, solidarity with the poor, and self-sacrifice—far from the worldly power of Herod's world.

Which king is worthy of our worship?

When the Magi finally came to the place where Jesus and his parents were living, they offered him costly gifts. These men were not playing the worship games of which many of us are guilty—these gifts of gold and precious spices nearly cost the Magi their lives.

In such a context, our worship must be reborn. The wise men show us what happens when someone catches even a glimpse of the matchless Christ. He is indeed worthy of all honor, glory, and praise. We will travel across the world to meet him, confront dominant world systems, and give our all for our King.

THE STORY THAT CHANGES EVERYTHING

It has been beautiful to see people in our communities worship in such a way. Whoever we are and wherever we find ourselves, we are learning to worship with the wise men, traveling across the world to bring the gift of ourselves—our presence, our labor, our money, our love—to hungry, thirsty, sick people who need Jesus—all in worship of the King.

Our eyes are being opened. The empire that we have been fueling with our time, attention, and money is not the kingdom of Jesus. What might happen if, at Advent and throughout the year, all of God's people worshiped more like the Magi? What transformation would occur as God's people moved across the globe loving Jesus with our time, attention, and money?

The characters of the Advent drama are each threads in a rich, textured tapestry of worship. It is a story that is still unfolding, a story that inspires prophetic poetry of worshiping communities all over the world. A story about the radical solidarity of Jesus worshipers who commit themselves to standing with the least of these in the far corners of the world and in the midst of injustice. A story about passionate resistance from people who refuse to be enveloped by another empire's demands and instead live simply and faithfully for their King. A story about faithful worship at the feet of a glorified and yet humble King.

As followers of Jesus, our options are clear: we can inhabit the story of a corrupt world and bow to a counterfeit king, or we can enter the story of God and celebrate the world's one true Lord.

If we choose the former, we need not change anything. Christmas—and the rest of our lives—will look much the same as now. But if we choose to enter the story of God, we choose to enter the greatest story ever, the story that changes everything. When we enter the Advent story, we cannot remain silent!

Like Mary, we will sing to our redeeming God. Like Elizabeth, we will open our lives and homes to others. Like Joseph, we will obey without regard to the cost. Like the shepherds, we will leave our busyness to worship Christ. Like the Magi, we will confront anything that stands in the way of our worship—from worldly empires to our own fears.

We will celebrate, sing, dance, pray, meditate, and love our way into a story that is of great joy for all people. Christmas changed the world the day Jesus was born in a cold, dark stable; Christmas will change the world again.

CHAPTER 4

SPEND LESS

THE STORY OUR MONEY TELLS

We have inserted ourselves into the birth story and opened our hearts to the possibility of a deeper, fuller worship experience—not only at Christmas but beyond. Jesus has become the reason for our season but also the reason for everything we do. We hang on his every word. So when Jesus said, "People try to serve both God and money—but you can't. *You must choose one or the other*,"[1] what are we to do with this? Is it possible to turn the tables on this age-old struggle? We may be face to face with a newborn Jesus who brings us to our knees in worship, but spending less at Christmas may still seem like an impossibly hard next step.

Christmas is a season of excess. It is difficult to walk against the crowd who seem to want nothing more than to "eat, drink, and be merry" . . . and then do it all again. Spending less requires us to plan, research, and cultivate relationships—pursuits that are more taxing than flipping through the latest catalog or bingeing online.

However, as we choose to go against the cultural

flow, it is important to remember that spending less on Christmas presents doesn't mean we love our friends and family any less. In fact, we will often find that those to whom we give creative, personal gifts will see and sense our love—and perhaps God's—more clearly than ever before.

GIVING BEAUTIFULLY

"Spend less" is an ambiguous goal. Spend less than last year? Spend less than my neighbor? Spend less than the average American, who spends almost one thousand dollars on Christmas gifts? Yes and no.

The key is to ask such questions aloud and then be willing to engage the emerging tensions. How much is too much? How can you tell when you have too much? Who determines what you "need"? The line between excessive wealth and simplicity may be hard to discern—but it's hard to escape the conclusion that nearly all of us have too much.

There is no simple formula here (and beware the pride of thinking your answers to these questions are the only answers). But simple, specific questions are a great place to start. Your answers will involve many variables, but ask God to help you sift through them with an honest and humble heart.

Do I need another car? If so, does it have to be a new car? Is Christmas the right time to give or receive such an extravagant gift? How much house is too much? How many pairs of shoes are too many? When did I last wear *that* pair anyway? Should I ask for a leather jacket for Christmas? How many coats do I need? John the Baptist says if you have two coats, then you should give the second away. I wonder—and maybe rationalize— did he mean two coats of the same style or purpose? I have a raincoat, a ski jacket, a leather coat, an overcoat, a windbreaker, multiple sport coats, a light coat, and a heavy coat, and I may have a few others.

The challenge is to balance our desires with the needs in our communities and the rest of the world. This means that shopping will become less about entertainment and more about necessities. It means that researching purchases may become more complicated than simply seeking the greatest value or the highest visibility.

What about community consequences? Are you supporting businesses that treat their employees well or advocate for causes that you believe in? Do you agree with the ways the product is advertised? Are they using sexual appeal to sell the product? Do children see these advertisements?

What about environmental consequences? Was your television manufactured in an area where factories are routinely ignoring environmental guidelines? Is the product recyclable or reusable? Was the product shipped halfway across the globe? If so, the environmental cost is significant.

Two local churches partnered to rescue several refugees in Rwanda who needed only bus fare to escape to Nairobi and relative safety. What seemed like an insurmountable amount (fifty-five dollars per person) was little more than what some in the group spent on diet soda each month. Within days, the money was collected. Within weeks, the refugees were out of Rwanda. According to their new church in Nairobi, these rescued ones have injected new life into their worship services with the loud and grateful singing.

We must also ask what story we are telling our children. Is it healthy to give our children whatever they want? Does it build character? Many of us are guilty of giving our children too much. Many children are completely overwhelmed with gifts, the sheer volume of which distracts them from the celebration of Jesus. A family in Austin, Texas, chose to radically change the way they experience Christmas, and the first step was slashing their spending budget. They were nervous and unsure how their children would respond, but the true beauty of Christmas changed them. They described their new way of giving this way:

> When we first talked with the boys about changing our Christmas budget, they were a little disappointed. But looking back, I don't remember seeing any of that on Christmas Day. David and I are so grateful for Advent Conspiracy. We knew things didn't feel right, that there was something askew with our Christmases—but we couldn't pinpoint exactly what was wrong. I remember thinking something must be missing. Maybe there was something more . . .

Indeed there is: more joy, more relief, more meaning. The wonderful surprise of this conspiracy is how much more we enjoy Christmas when we choose less. This stands in stark contrast to the message we hear each December. Unfortunately for many, Christmas is more about getting what we want than giving what people need. Is this the tradition we want to pass down to the next generation?

IS SPENDING LESS WRONG?

Perhaps you've heard something like this: "Surely you don't really want Americans to spend less; you must understand that our economy relies on consumer spending. If Americans do not spend, then Americans will ultimately lose their jobs and suffer. Do you really want to cause suffering by asking Christians to spend less?"

At first glance, this circular argument seems to make sense. For instance, when our movement first caught the eye of the national media, such questions were regularly posed: Is this really helpful (and patriotic) to suggest that we spend less? Of course, such questions immediately led to interesting discussions about how "patriotic" it is to plunge deeper and deeper into personal debt every Christmas. But this is only a portion of what we are suggesting. Of course it is ridiculous to run up your credit card debt in the name of Jesus' birth. Please, let's not blame that on him. But there is another aspect of this worth considering.

Spending less does not mean spending nothing. Rather, we strive to thoughtfully evaluate what we support with our spending, and we allow our spending to support products, people, and causes that are worthy of being supported.

SPEND LESS, EXCEPT WHEN YOU SHOULD SPEND MORE

Suppose you have a two-year-old television. Do you now need the newest, thinnest version to help you celebrate the birth of Christ? Do we need to spend more on products that aren't necessary, especially products whose hidden personal, communal, and environmental costs are so high?

Yet sometimes we purchase something in order to keep someone employed. In a desperately poor Calcutta slum where young women are often forced to become sex workers because they lack any other options, a new business is blossoming that teaches these young girls to make beautiful handmade journals. Suppose you already have a journal. Do you need to buy yourself three new journals handmade by former prostitutes in Calcutta? Will that help you celebrate the birth of Christ? You might choose to buy a box of journals, but it becomes more about the girls than the journals themselves. We spend less at Christmas, except when we should spend more.

In Buenos Aires there is a pastor in a shantytown where homes are little more than mud huts. His church members make thousands of gorgeous leather Bible covers that are sold in America and used to support these indigenes in Argentina. Most of us don't need a new Bible cover, but when we choose to purchase one, we can be grateful knowing that God is using our money for the greater good of his kingdom. And who knows, perhaps we did need a fresh reminder to read his Word.

There are times we will want to spend more to help others keep gainful employment, feed their children, and get basic medical care. The question we must ask as we spend is: Who is our money supporting? Do we want our Christmas spending to support slavery or child labor or the dehumanizing practices of corrupt regimes? Do we want to support corporations that exploit workers in sweatshops and pay them less than a living wage? If not, we'll spend a little more time researching the products we purchase, even looking for those certified as Fair Trade.

Asking questions like these will stimulate prayerful conversations that can lead to thoughtful adjustments in our spending. Such decisions might help us eliminate spending from our budgets that brings harm to ourselves, our neighbors, or our world.

THE PROBLEM IS NOT CAPITALISM

It is possible to spend compassionately and responsibly regardless of our economic system. When capitalism unwittingly marries unbridled Western individualism, however, catastrophe results. In such a cultural system, every person becomes a society of one, making a mockery of the idea of a nation of liberty and freedom. The thinking behind such a warped approach puts personal profit and convenience above all else. As long as it is "good" for me, I choose not to consider the effect of my choices on others. Ironically, such a lifestyle is rarely, if ever, "good" for me as I unwittingly contribute to problems that will ripple through the world in which I still live. And some of these choices are clearly not "good" for others as they may devastate the lives of hundreds or even thousands of people.

How strange and sad it is that debt and consumerism reach their pinnacle on the morning we celebrate the birth of Jesus—the Savior who came to liberate us from these things. When we give gifts without regard to "the least of these," it reflects a brand of capitalism gone wrong.

And with this, we all lose.

The Creator of heaven and earth had something very different in mind for his creation. The Bible tells us to approach life and finances with an open hand: "The objective is not to go under so others will have some relief; the objective is to use this opportunity today to supply their needs out of your abundance. One day it may be the other way around, and they will need to supply your needs from what they have. That's equality."[2]

THE LOVE OF MONEY

The love of money, which the apostle Paul called "the root of all sorts of evil,"[3] plagues all people, even (and sometimes especially) people of faith. Televangelists want more satellites; pastors and rabbis and imams want bigger houses of worship. And those who listen to these teachers are no less susceptible to the tug and lure of "more." We want bigger cars, homes, and a corner office with a view. Why should we spend less and give more?

In the first century, the apostle Paul employed pointed rhetoric to warn his friends about excess: "But those who chase riches are constantly falling into temptation and snares. They are regularly caught by their own stupid and harmful desires, dragged down and pulled under into ruin and destruction."[4] Some theologians and pastors try to justify financial excess as a blessing from God. They crave God's stamp of approval on their chosen lifestyles and view their abundance as a reward for personal righteousness. They think, "If God doesn't like what he sees, why did he gift me so richly?"

"Dear Pastor: If you don't get this message, then call me. I am going to ask for some money and toys from Santa (for other kids). I'm going to ask Santa to also send food and water to those kids. I also have my own bucket of money to give them." (letter from a five-year-old)

Now, does God bless some with uncommon wealth? Clearly, even the Scriptures hold such examples. But is wealth alone an indication of his favor? Hardly. There is so much to this discussion, but one point is painfully clear: there is inherent danger in the pursuit and accumulation of wealth at all costs.

And this "infectious greed," as one former chairman of the Federal Reserve put it, is not so easily cured. It certainly cannot be eliminated through rivers of new legislation flowing out of Washington. Our economy and our society have accepted radical greed as the norm, and each of us somehow justifies the suffering of others that our lifestyle causes. The only sure remedy is a change of heart, and the best place to begin is at the feet of the newborn Jesus.

Are we willing to rethink the way we use our wealth? Do we long to rediscover the beauty of true giving? The Judeo-Christian tradition offers clear direction about what we willingly offer back to God to use for his greater purposes. The Hebrew Scriptures talk a great deal about giving a tithe (10 percent of income), while the New Testament opens the floodgates and pushes us toward boundary-busting generosity. Reflecting on the meaning of God's gifts to us, the apostle Paul says, "You will be made rich in everything so that your generosity *will spill over in every direction.*"[5]

An Advent Conspiracy pastor in Pennsylvania experienced this in his congregation: "People in our church grabbed hold of the concept of spending less. People made Christmas simpler in order to worship fully. People gave relationally. A woman chose to ask her neighbors what their favorite charities were, and instead of giving them a typical gift, she donated to those agencies in their names. Christmas is becoming something different—and something better!"

Like Jesus, the twentieth-century author C. S. Lewis believed that the best way to break money's power is to give it away—yet he shrank from suggesting a rigid formula for giving. "I do not believe one can settle how much we ought to give," he wrote. Lewis continued:

> I am afraid the only safe rule is to give more than we can spare. In other words, if our expenditure on comforts, luxuries, amusements, etc., is up to the standard common among those with the same income as our own, we are probably giving away too little. If our charities do not at all pinch or hamper us, I should say they are too small. There ought to be things we should like to do and cannot do because our charitable expenditure excludes them.[6]

What would our world look like if people of faith began acting on Lewis's suggestion? What would happen in our nation if both executives and laborers began practicing a kind of generosity that "pinched"? How would our neighborhoods be transformed if we gave more than we could spare?

This Advent season, what would it take for us to actually give it a try?

A FEW IDEAS TO CONSIDER

- Get into the habit of asking a few more questions before spending your money.
- Develop a thoughtful approach to the histories of the products and companies who you purchase from.
- Enter such a process with humility, and resist the potential pride in thinking *your way* of approaching such a complicated matter is the only way. This conspiracy will only grow with winsome voices calling others to new places and thoughts.
- Set your budget; know your limit. (If it's early enough, start saving for a debt-free celebration.)
- Before you start buying, consider each person on your list. Think about your relationship and what significance it brings to your life.
- Consider your core values and whether what you are buying reflects those values.
- Consider drawing names, giving one less gift than last year, or maybe two?
- Talk openly and early with your family. You will be surprised how quickly they begin to understand your motives. In our experiences at each of our

churches, it is often the children who let go of hyperconsumption before the grown-ups.

At the end of the day, we hope that your celebration of the birth of the Liberating King is focused less on what you spent and more on giving from a place of true worship.

CHAPTER 5

GIVE MORE

THE GIFT OF MEANINGFUL CONNECTION

This invitation to push back against overspending and overconsumption during Advent resonates deeply with people of various backgrounds and economic realities. We've grown weary of the holiday ad campaigns that seem to start earlier and earlier each year. Kids struggle to find the connection between their Christmas wish list and the story of Jesus' birth. Parents search for even a fleeting moment of worship. Many of us reach the end of each Advent season with an aching emptiness. Sifting through piles of things we don't need and may never use, something deep inside tells us we missed it—whatever it is our soul longs for this time of year.

And now, when we're invited to rebel against some of this craziness by spending less, it simply seems right. But then we're being encouraged to give more? That sure sounds like a contradiction, doesn't it?

Maybe not.

We can all agree that there is still something deeply moving and beautiful about certain gifts. Think about the most memorable Christmas present you've ever received. What was it that touched you? Why do you still remember it to this day? You probably aren't remembering a pair of new cars sitting in the driveway with big red bows on top or a huge diamond bracelet hanging on the tree (does that happen outside of those December commercials?). For most of us, the special gift we best remember is a different kind of gift—a relational gift.

The best gifts celebrate a relationship. In the office of a successful man who attends one of our churches sits a rudimentary hand-painted frame. The corners aren't perfect. The primary colors are a jolt to the rest of his office décor. But is it a work of art? Just ask him. For it was made by his children when the Advent Conspiracy was just beginning. Since then, they have both graduated college and moved out on their own. But it was their effort and love that put the frame together. And they are the ones who glued a photo of them with their dad right in the middle. Such a gift is priceless for many reasons, but mostly because it is personal. All these years later, when this father looks at that particular gift, he's reminded of children who love him and a relationship that he's still celebrating.

It sounds so obvious, yet we seem to have drifted

from this liberating, straightforward truth: the Father gave his one and only Son. God's answer for the world's problems has never been material things. God did not give us more stuff—even good stuff like work, food, or health. He gave us himself. The most priceless and personal gift of all.

This simple truth is why giving is still a good way to celebrate the birth of Jesus. It also points to a way out of the chaos of consumerism that Christmas has become, taking us back to the joy that can still be found at the heart of this story. Our giving can actually reflect in some small way the power and beauty of God coming into our world as one of us.

THE INCARNATION

Incarnation is a word that doesn't even make it into our Bibles, but the writers of Scripture describe it so powerfully that we cannot deny its reality. The Incarnation is the moment when Jesus, the divine Son of the Eternal Father, entered our story as a human baby. Only someone with an especially large ideological axe to grind would attempt to deny the existence of a man named Jesus who lived in Palestine two thousand years ago. And while this is certainly an important aspect of the Incarnation—that Jesus lived on this earth as a human—we know it means more than a simple historical fact.

An eighty-four-year-old grandmother apologized to her family for not being able to give lavish gifts on her limited income. This did not, however, keep her from giving her eighty-five dollars to the Christmas offering.

The miracle of Christmas is the infinite becoming finite—an infant fully human and still fully God. This profound truth lies at the heart of the historic Christian faith. It unites Catholics and Protestants, Baptists and Episcopalians, house churches and megachurches. All Christians confess that Jesus is God. While we could refer to famous church councils in the centuries that followed his time on earth or quote from the creeds of our faith, this truth was declared much earlier.

The Gospel of John begins with this sentence: "In the beginning was the Word"—John's term for his friend Jesus in these opening lines to this eyewitness account—"and the Word was with God, and the Word was God. He was with God in the beginning. Through him all things were made; without him nothing was made that has been made."[1] John tells us Jesus not only made us, he formed the world around us and cast the planets around that world and spaced out the galaxies beyond those planets.

Unfortunately, these familiar words have grown stale to many. We seem to rush past the mind-stretching claims being made in this opening paragraph—and when we do, we miss the power of John's words. Listen to the same verses from a different translation that is still faithful to the original text: "Before time itself was measured, the Voice was speaking. The Voice was and is God. This *celestial* Word remained ever present with the Creator; His speech shaped the entire cosmos."[2] That's who Jesus is—the one whose speech shaped the entire cosmos. John has no problem telling us that Jesus of Nazareth is more than a gifted rabbi and good friend. Jesus is more than an extraordinary human being—Jesus was and is the Son of God.

So when we read a few verses later that "the Word became flesh and made his dwelling among us,"[3] we understand that to be the miracle of the Incarnation. John is unambiguous. When he writes of the Word becoming flesh, it means just what we think it means. God became bone and skin and guts. It's not just that Jesus is God—it's that Jesus, as God, chose to become one of us. That's the Incarnation. The one who spoke galaxies into existence, in the words of author Alan Hirsch, "moved into our neighborhood in an act of humble love the likes of which the world has never known."[4]

Jesus as the Incarnation of God is our fullest and best understanding of God. Jesus himself said, "The Father and I are one,"[5] and that when we've seen him, we've seen the Father.[6] What does all this mean? Because of the Incarnation, the infinite God becomes more tangible, more approachable, and more (though never completely) comprehensible. It's because of Jesus that we know who the Eternal God of the universe is and what he's really like. Talk about a relational gift! But it gets even better.

THE STORY HAS FOREVER CHANGED

The Incarnation is what we celebrate when we gather for worship. It's what we celebrate at the communion table. It's the very good news we proclaim to a world that has forgotten what very good news sounds like. God was here in flesh and blood as the fulfillment of a promise—and that gives us real hope. In the strong words of theologian N. T. Wright, "Jesus exploded into the life of ancient Israel—the life of the whole world, in fact—not as a teacher of timeless truths, nor as a great moral example, but as the one through whose life, death, and resurrection God's rescue operation was put into effect, and the cosmos turned its great corner at last."[7] Apart from the Incarnation, we would never fully know the depths to which we are loved or the lengths to which God can be trusted. That's what we celebrate each Christmas.

When we give relationally during the Advent season, this is what we remember: it's an opportunity to worship as we remind each other of the gift that was given for our sake.

LET'S ADMIT SOMETHING

One of the big pressures each Christmas season is coming up with gift ideas. And for some, that pressure seems to increase when we decide not to buy Uncle Murray that sweater he was never going to wear anyway. Now what? We have to be creative? We have to think? This is usually about the time some of us get a little fearful that we're not going to come up with anything meaningful. Because here's our little admission: we don't see ourselves as all that creative. So where do we start? Before you buy the hot-glue gun or take a class in woodworking, let's begin by again taking our cue from the story of Jesus.

As others have pointed out, the Incarnation suggests, in very practical terms, what it means to give ourselves to one another.[8] Let's quickly look at four aspects of what happened when God gave us his one and only Son.

God gave us his presence.

In the Incarnation, God drew close in a very specific, historical way. In Matthew's account of Jesus' birth, he takes us back to the words of Isaiah, stating "they will call him Immanuel."[9] He then explains that this is a Hebrew name that means "God with us." Many of us remember to repeat this name at Christmas each year and tell each other what it means—but do we allow it to permeate the way we live during the Advent season? Is it possible that even our gift giving could be drenched with this beautiful moment when God gave us his presence in a unique, flesh-and-blood way? The apostle Paul writes that Jesus is the image of the invisible God.[10] God had a face and a voice, and he lived with real people. There's something incredibly tangible about God's gift. What can that teach us about the way we give Christmas gifts?

Our world is increasingly fractured, yet we often mask this distance with a kind of pseudo-community—we call; we text; we Facebook, Tweet, Instagram; and the list goes on. These can be important ways to keep in touch, but they can never replace the flesh-and-blood aspect of a relationship. We were made to be with each other. To hear another voice, to see another face, to hold another hand . . . it's one of the ways we are reminded that we are not alone.

When we make time to be with someone, it's a gift—a relational gift. The conscious giving of our time and presence to another is not a new concept, but it is a neglected one. Consider how you can creatively express to that friend or family member how much you want to *be* with them. For example, a young man buys his father a pound of coffee beans with one stipulation: "Dad can only enjoy this gift with his grown son." And in the hours and days it will take to drink those cups of coffee, as that son listens to his dad tell stories and the two of them get reacquainted, what does that say to this father? He hears from his son: *I just want to be reminded of you and how you became the man that you are.* This is what it means to give your presence in simple but meaningful ways.

The gift of Jesus was personal.

Luke's account of the Christmas story includes that very famous angelic announcement: "Today, in the city of David, a Liberator has been born for you! He is the promised Anointed One, the Supreme Authority!"[11] A Savior has been born to *you*—a very personal gift! Over and over the Gospels demonstrate the relational nature of Jesus. He simply liked being with people.

Not only that, he intentionally cultivated those relationships. He paid attention. He listened. He noticed. He did everything that people in a hurry forget to do.

We've all received gifts that were, shall we say, less than personal (feel free to insert your own awkward example here). But the truth is, we've given gifts like that too. Generic, disposable gifts are not only a waste of money, but they practically scream, "I haven't thought about you in a long time, but I still felt obligated to give you something." Is that kind of giving moving us any closer to celebrating the story of Jesus?

Relational giving means that we pay attention to the other person. We think about who they are and what they care about.

A father and his teenage daughter were enjoying their last Christmas at home before she headed off to college the following summer. For him, the days were beginning to blur into weeks and the little girl he was bouncing on his lap just yesterday was going to leave tomorrow.

What did that father give his daughter that Christmas? Two beautiful blank journals with these instructions: she was to fill one, and he'd fill the other. During the next year, which would include her final days of high school, an all-too-brief summer, and her first semester away from home, they both committed to writing: thoughts about leaving home, questions and fears, frustrations with over-protective parenting, what it meant to let go, and how it feels to watch your child become an adult. The next Christmas, they'd exchange their journals.

Two empty journals for Christmas—that's what a daughter got from her dad? How impersonal such a gesture might appear at first glance—and how inadequate! But no gift could have been more relational, more personal, and no other gift would stand a chance of being appreciated so warmly or remembered for so long.

His gift was costly.

There is an aspect of the Incarnation that is God becoming a servant. In places like the book of Philippians, we see that Jesus intentionally took on the form of a serv-ant.[12] He did not force his way into our world as the powerful King he truly is. Instead, Jesus chose to enter the story in the humblest of ways. As Hirsch reminds us, "This [truth] now commits us to servanthood and humility in our relationships with each other and the world."[13]

Of course, his humility did not stop there, for it led to the cross. In the words of Jesus himself, "Even the Son of Man came not to be served but to be a serv-ant—to offer His life as a ransom for others."[14]

The gift God gave us cost him everything. What does that mean for us as we now give to one another?

In practical terms, it means we must accept that relational giving will cost us. While not to the depths of what it cost Jesus to become human, much less the sacrifice of the cross, relational gifts will cost our time and energy. It would be easier to stop by the store or go online to buy something "in the ballpark."

Relational giving will also be risky at times. What if they don't like it? What if they don't understand our intent? What if they don't appreciate the time we put into expressing love for them? This too is a reflection of the Incarnation. Didn't Jesus give himself knowing full well that some would reject or misunderstand him?

We ought not to take this too far, or we'll succumb to the martyr complex that lurks just beneath the surface of many well-intentioned Christians. But part of relational giving is understanding that our heartfelt gifts simply might not be appreciated. Hopefully they will be, though, as often even the crustiest of hearts will soften with such personal gestures.

The gift is not about the giver but about the other. Such gifts, when given with this spirit of humility, drip with grace. Can you think of a better way to celebrate Jesus?

Consider a woman who, without her friend knowing it, asked this person's friends and family to each write a note or send a picture that celebrated that one beautiful life. Over the course of weeks, she began compiling a scrapbook with these photos, drawings, notes, letters, and poems of various lengths. Sometimes it took some friendly reminders to encourage participation. On Christmas Day the gift was truly a work of art. It was beautiful, of course, but the contents of this multilayered gift took much longer to truly appreciate. Imagine the tears of joy, the sometimes bittersweet memories, and the reflections of a life well lived as this friend slowly went through the book page by page on Christmas morning.

Here's the last detail: the woman who had assembled this whole project wasn't even there when her friend opened it! She thought it best for such a gift to be enjoyed in the privacy of family, so she asked them to present the gift on her behalf Christmas morning. There was no moment of triumph, no basking in the glory of her very generous gesture. For her, it really wasn't about that. It was a gift of love given in the spirit of her Savior who is himself a servant.

His gift bridged the gap.

This hints at one more difficult question often asked: *What if I can't be physically present with someone this Advent season?* Most of us have experienced the inability to spend time with someone because of distance or circumstance. What might our gift look like? Two young women gave their Nana, with whom they were not able to spend much time because of distance, a modest but most precious Christmas gift to celebrate that relationship. It consisted of a large mason jar full of colorful strips of paper—fifty-two of them to be exact. The instructions were simple. At the beginning of each week the following year, Nana was to randomly pull out one of the brightly-colored pieces of construction paper. On it she would find a story, handwritten by one or both great-granddaughters. That story would recount the time they had spent growing up with her loving care. "I remember you walking me around the pond and feeding the ducks . . ." a story might begin. It was a celebration of very personal moments this great-grandma had invested in these two young women. It was also a way to tell her they had not forgotten this relationship. In fact, they told her they too would remember and thank God in the coming year for their Nana as they looked ahead to more face-to-face moments together.

To hear this elderly woman tell it, Monday morning now became her favorite time of the week. A moment of nostalgia, yes, but a time of worship too. God was making this connection between generations vibrant with a mason jar full of construction paper. And a distance between loved ones was, in some ways, closed.

Such a gift takes time and thought. But we can do this! We can help each other get better at this. What a joy it is when a thought comes to mind of how you might serve and honor someone else. You'll hardly be able to wait until Christmas to give such a gift.

This is what awaits in this unlikely conspiracy you're being invited to join.

If we can resist the trap of giving easy gifts, and if

we can reject the assumption that giving expensive gifts or many gifts is the best way to express love, something else might begin to happen. We might experience moments of relational giving that our friends and family will care about and remember. Our kids will learn what it means to give gifts that are personal and meaningful. Our neighbors and coworkers and friends will watch us celebrate Christmas differently, and they'll hear the good news loud and clear through the seasonal static.

CHAPTER 6

LOVE ALL

MAKING A DIFFERENCE
HERE AND NOW

When the Advent Conspiracy was taking shape, some of us were part of a strategic team that was assessing the water crisis in Liberia. The handful of churches that first caught the vision of what could happen if we celebrated Christmas differently were committed to funneling some of our resources away from overconsumption and toward those who might be considered "the least of these" around the world.

Sensing that our five churches could start to make a difference, we journeyed to Africa with a team from Living Water International, a nonprofit that digs freshwater wells in places around the world most of us don't know exist. At times it didn't seem like we'd be able to reach some of these villages. Bouncing from rut to rut for hours in the back of a Land Rover makes us painfully aware how far removed we are from the struggles of many in this world.

We stopped at a village that, like many others, welcomed us with beautiful smiles and open arms. We were led through tall grasses, away from the village, to what they referred to as their "well." If it was a well, it was not like any well we'd ever seen. It sat next to a swamp that leached untold disease into the water from which families drew their water every day. This stagnant gray-green pool infested with insects was all these people had. Even as we talked with the village elders, women would casually brush away the film that clung to the top of this water as they filled their pots.

Looking at this water dripping with disease, it seemed all too real. Surely God was leading us. Not only could we push back against the hyperconsumerism of our own culture, we could also begin to heal the disease that was seeping into this one. And as a result, we could share the story of Jesus, the living water. Everything seemed to be coming together in this one moment.

We listened as the village chief told us of those who had died recently because of illnesses that came from drinking this water. Standing with us in our small circle was a man whose son had just died from a waterborne disease. The faces on these elders were somber and hopeless, almost resigned to the fact that burying their children would always be a part of their lives.

We knew that in several weeks our churches would be taking Christmas offerings. We knew that by partnering with Living Water International, in a couple of months this village would not have to rely on that well ever again. For us this was good news, and we wanted to share it with the chief and his elders.

When this message of hope was delivered—with great passion by a translator from the area who was as excited as we were—the weathered face of this honorable elder remained impassive. He simply stared at us.

Even our translator was puzzled by this lack of emotion. When he asked the chief if he understood what this would mean for his people, the answer was unforgettable: "Others have made promises in the name of this Jesus, but they were never kept." Here was a man whose hope had dried up and blown away because others had made promises in the name of Jesus that they'd never bothered to keep.

THE REACTION SAYS IT ALL

Somewhere along the way, this man and his village were probably "told the right things" about Jesus: how God loved the world so much that he gave his only Son. Apparently they were also told by well-meaning Christians that help was on the way, that someone had noticed their struggle. But no one showed up. Nothing changed. Kids were still dying in the village, and the name of Jesus had been dragged through the mud.

While sitting at a fast-food restaurant, a third grader was expressing her hurt that there were kids around the world without clean drinking water. When an employee overheard her, the restaurant decided that 50 percent of the proceeds for one day last fall would go toward the crisis. On that single day, $4,451.64 was raised toward the girl's goal of $15,000 to build a well in Zimbabwe. She is currently at $8,000.

Is it possible that someone thought it would be enough to tell the people of this village that God loved them without feeling compelled to be an active agent of that love? Sometimes we are so focused on what happens after people die that we don't pay attention to the life they're living now. Author Scot McKnight warns us that the church suffers when it treats humans as souls made for eternity instead of whole persons made for now and eternity.[1] Of course, it's not just the church that suffers—it's everyone who might have been helped by a church intent on participating in God's plan to bring justice and hope to this world. When Jesus said he came to bring good news to the poor, he meant it.[2]

Jesus was more than an activist, however. Ready to save people's bodies now *and* for eternity, Jesus taught us to pray for daily bread *and* for our sins to be forgiven. When he spoke of the poor in the Gospel of Luke, there was a deeper, spiritual meaning.[3] The good news of the kingdom is for anyone in dire need of God—even those who might assume they'll never be helped. Soldiers, beggars, the religious elite, tax collectors, rich people, prostitutes, the working class, lepers—Jesus brought good news to everyone.

THE HEART OF THE CHRISTMAS STORY

God came to the poor—in other words, to each of us. The apostle Paul reminds us that "He set aside His infinite riches and was born into the lowest circumstance so that you may gain great riches through His humble poverty."[4]

What does this mean? Jesus gave up the glory of heaven to be born into a sin-scarred world. That glorious night in Bethlehem, every day of his life, and in the deadly pain of the cross, Jesus became poor for our sake. Jesus entered our poverty so we would no longer be poor. The priceless gift of a restored relationship with God and others is now offered to those who could never afford it. The outrageous wealth of his righteousness is credited to those who don't deserve it. To those of us who are poor, this is very good news.

But is it still relevant news? Can Christmas still change the world? We've discovered over this last decade that the answer is a resounding yes! But how exactly does that happen? How can Christmas and the way we celebrate it still change the world?

As desperate people who've experienced the righteous wealth of God, it is now our turn to model his generosity by sharing our wealth with those in need. Christmas is our chance to move closer to those in crisis, not further away. It is our time to notice those who are normally ignored. In short, it is our turn to love as we have been loved. In practical terms, our love must include caring for the poor in our midst.

Over and over we see Jesus teaching that God is on the side of the impoverished, even when no one else is. Throughout the Gospels, he raises the status of those the world mistreats and marginalizes—people who are deemed hopeless and beyond help. Jesus is clear: he expects his followers to do the same.

There's no way around it: Jesus calls us to love and care for the poor.

At Christmas, one of the things that should distinguish a Christ follower is a love that reaches out to the hungry and thirsty and sick and imprisoned. Such giving is an act of true worship. There is a close connection between how we treat each other and how we treat God. In Matthew's Gospel, Jesus says that whatever we do for one of the least of his brothers and sisters, we do for him.[5] God takes these acts of love (or moments of rejection) very personally.

And why wouldn't he? Jesus himself was poor. He chose to be born into the poverty of a family struggling beneath the heel of Imperial Rome. Writer Scott Bessenecker suggests that "the very first statement Jesus ever voiced about his concern for the poor, oppressed, marginalized people was when he cried out as one of them—eyes shut tight, mouth open wide, wailing, kicking . . . It was one of the most profound acts of solidarity with the poor he could make."[6] For all of the other aspects of his Advent we celebrate each year, let us not forget this part of the story: "When God voted with his birth, he voted for the poor."[7]

OUR TURN

We cannot allow the broken and vulnerable to become invisible. Which brings us back to how Christmas can still change the world. Let's return to Jesus' words in Matthew 25: *"You shall be richly rewarded,* for when I was hungry, you fed Me. And when I was thirsty, you gave Me something to drink. I was alone as a stranger, and you welcomed Me *into your homes and into your lives.* I was naked, and you gave Me clothes to wear; I was sick, and you tended to My needs; I was in prison, and you comforted Me."[8] These are very simple acts of service being described—giving someone something to eat or drink, welcoming them, clothing them, visiting them. Simple as they are, these gifts matter very much to Jesus—and to those in need. So why not start there? Sometimes we will be led to huge, global strategies (more on that in the next chapter), but it's usually the simple, commonsense acts of love that make the difference.

Think of a single parent "adopted" anonymously by someone at church, provided with toys for the kids, groceries, gas cards—that's the world being changed. Think of a family that decides to serve in a local shelter—the poor are cared for and the family members' hearts become a bit more like God's.

Picture entire churches deciding that some of the money they are saving by giving relationally and resisting cultural norms should be given to the "least of these" in our communities and world—that's when Christmas still makes a difference. Businesses find ways to give to these causes. Instead of sending a gift basket to their clients, they send a gift card representing money given to the digging of a well in Zimbabwe in honor of that client. Once they hear the story, now they choose to get involved. Students get creative about giving to other kids they may never meet. The presents around the tree aren't stacked quite so high, but the stories of worship and love grow richer and deeper. In many churches, including ours, young children tell their parents and grandparents they would like that "one present," yes, but to then give the rest to kids they don't know halfway around the world. People of all ages are finding themselves, with generous hearts, offering their time, money, and selves to others because they are compelled by the love of God.

Through this kind of radical but practical giving, we are transformed by the Advent story. But make no mistake: the changes that occur are not simply about us. God is up to something in his world. When God's people serve the poor in humble, generous ways, the story of Jesus is told again and again. The poor in our world will be touched by God through how we choose to celebrate Christmas.

Of course, as Reggie McNeal reminds us, "God is the One doing the heavy lifting!"[9] Through his trustworthy Spirit, God is sending us into a broken but beautiful world on which he will never give up. When we show up and love in the name of God, God shows up. That's part of the mystery of partnering with Jesus in the work he is still doing.

In this decidedly cynical world, where far too many people have heard far too many empty words, the way we love others makes a difference—whether the others live in the third world or the third house down the street.

A BEAUTIFUL BODY

We still believe that each of these beautiful acts of love can combine together to form a movement that changes the world. The Advent Conspiracy isn't simply about individuals or single churches giving people a sense of who Jesus is—it's about the entire body of Christ at work in the world. As we worship more, spend less, give more, and love all, something begins to form that is greater than any single person or denomination. We celebrate other ministries. We focus on places in our own communities and around the world where we can combine our efforts with our brothers and sisters. As we love our neighbors *and* one another, the kingdom of God grows and the world takes notice.[10]

Instead of the adult siblings exchanging gifts, we take the money and give to a charity of our choosing that we are passionate about. At the Christmas family dinner, each sibling tells why this cause has meaning in their life, usually done with great passion, tears, and profound meaning.

This is why we suggest that each organization—from churches to student ministries to parachurch groups—gather an offering of the money saved by giving relationally and resisting consumerism. We want to be clear: we don't want your money. Not a dime of what any organization collects has ever been given to this thing we call the Advent Conspiracy. Instead, we ask that each organization take whatever money it raises and prayerfully give it to those who need it most.

We also ask participants to consider what it would mean to partner with others of like heart and mind. It is amazing to see how much good can be done in the world when we join others. In 2006, only five churches participated in this conspiracy and they collected nearly half a million dollars! Because of the nature of this movement, it is difficult to track just how much has been given away over these last years. But a conservative estimate of the money raised toward the water crisis has reached more than 16.2 million dollars. And this figure doesn't include the millions of dollars that have been raised for other causes around the globe! Now, again we ask, can you imagine what would happen if even more churches joined together in telling the world about Jesus' birth *and* in living out the story of his sacrificial love?

The poor and vulnerable and outcast will be seen and heard and touched and fed—not out of some class-based guilt but as an act of worship. We must not forget that. The good news of the gospel is for all people, including us. We are all poor and blind and imprisoned. We are the ones who have been given this lavish gift of life with God, and now we are called to enter this broken world and love differently. When we do, Christmas can still change the world.

A few months after Christmas we received word from Living Water International that the funds we had collected in December were now being used to dig wells in Liberia. It was happening because children on the other side of the world saved their pennies, families celebrated Christmas differently, students creatively pooled their resources, and churches took offerings. People in western Africa whom these folks would never meet this side of heaven were about to be loved in a practical and biblical way. Cup after cup of clean water would be given in the name of Jesus. Who knows where the conversations might lead?

The first well was dug for a village that used to drink from a swamp, and for a chief who had given up on the name of Jesus.

A LASTING LEGACY

CHAPTER 7

WHAT IF?

W hat if the Advent is bigger than we dare imagine? The story of God's Son entering our world is the point of our worship and celebration each Christmas. Because of his great love, God moved into the neighborhood, and we now have hope. But the Incarnation is not something to be celebrated only once a year. The story is bigger than that—and it's still being written.

The clear teaching of Scripture shows that we are being sent into this broken world to both *tell* the great story of God's love and to *live* it. Our lives are to give others a picture of our Savior. As the apostle Paul reminds us, we are "representatives of the . . . Liberating King."[1]

By trusting in his Spirit who lives in us, we can be to a hurting world God's presence and beauty and glory and power in bigger ways than we ever thought possible. God is *still* moving into the neighborhood! The Incarnation isn't about only the *one* glorious moment in history when Jesus walked this earth—it's also about a God who still wants to make an appearance in this world through his followers.

Can we even begin to imagine what would happen if the followers of Jesus around the world started to live this truth? What would happen if we decided not to simply celebrate the Advent of Christ but to combat the leading cause of death in a practical way?

What if, together, we did something about the water crisis?

We don't have to walk but a few feet to spin a knob and have clean water for drinking, bathing, watering the lawn and garden (and kids, if yours are anything like ours), washing the dog and car and boat . . . it is shocking to think about how much of our water we watch simply run off.

Years ago in Liberia we met people who were collecting drinking water from the same cesspool that had killed family members the week before. Since then, we have seen that same story play out across other places in Africa and also Central America and India. We've encountered countless women and children who walk for miles to fill and carry twenty liters or more of water each day. Stagnant, disease-infested pond water. Sludge. Mud. Sewage-runoff water. According to the World Water Council, 1.1 billion people lack access to safe drinking water, 2.6 billion people lack adequate sanitation, and 88 percent of all sickness is attributable to inadequate water or sanitation.[2]

Let's confront that reality again: over six thousand children die every day from diarrhea-related diseases alone.[3] That is roughly 1.4 million children who die each year. As we saw in the previous chapter, each statistic is always someone's daughter, someone's son. If they aren't dying, they are trudging to cesspools or polluted public taps for water. In Africa and Asia, women and children walk an average of nearly four miles to collect this water.[4] Can you imagine the time spent walking, waiting, pumping, and returning home with (on average) forty-four pounds of water on your back or head? Being relieved of the burden of collecting and drinking unclean water gives youths (young girls especially) the ability to learn skills in school that will help them escape poverty. It reduces the amount of infant and toddler deaths, increases the productivity of adults, and extends the life of the elderly.[5] And it reduces incidents of rape and the dangers of human trafficking, for it is often young girls who travel these distances unprotected to gather the diseased water. By providing sustainable water sources for the entire community, darkness is pushed back in so many different ways, and hope has a chance.

Clean water for every person in the world. This is our dream, and yes, it's a big one. We are about to officially invite you to join us in that dream. Of course, the important thing is to listen to where and how God is leading you. But then this: *dream big.*

Three high school girls organized an initiative that raised awareness at their high school about the global water crisis. It all revolved around a single drop of water. From videos that played throughout lunch hour to a benefit concert to T-shirts that invited their fellow students to "be a dropout," they raised enough money for a well to be dug in West Africa.

If you are called to address the horrors of sex trafficking or to invest in an educational initiative, to feed the hungry or serve the least of these—near or far—in any number of ways, then by all means, answer that call.

But then invite others to join you and us in this Advent Conspiracy and see what happens.

Let's dream big.

EXCHANGING CONSUMPTION FOR COMPASSION

Together we are greater than we are apart. The Advent of Christ is an opportunity to declare to the world that

God has given us the greatest gift. Advent Conspiracy exists to help the church awaken, realign with God's movement, and worship Jesus wholly at Christmas— and thus be transformed by the God of Advent.

What if, in the coming years, Christ followers around the world started a countercultural movement that reached far beyond a few days each December? What if we resisted the empire of "more" even as our worship echoed throughout the year? What if the story of God drawing near compelled us to love those living on the margins of our world? What if we joined together—across lines that often separate us—to serve both local communities and remote villages in the name of Jesus? Perhaps we could reclaim the story of Christmas, and the world would once again take notice.

To those entering the conspiracy, we ask you now to bring this dream to a reality. Consider new collaborations with others in your community as together you serve those in your midst. Can you imagine what might happen if people in your group or church partnered with others across the city who are longing to celebrate this Christmas differently? How might the *world* be different next year? How might *you* be different?

As previously mentioned, part of our very big

dream is to end the global water crisis. What if the followers of Jesus joined together to do just that? Perhaps, in a sign of solidarity, you might consider designating even a portion of your Christmas offering to help fund sustainable water, sanitation, and hygiene projects around the world? In addition to other areas you might be led to support, this very basic need will open up new opportunities for people to live longer and better lives. Surely this too is a part of our gospel story. As we strive toward equality in just the basic necessities of life, life will abound. God will abound. His kingdom will advance. Let us never forget: Jesus is the water of life. He values life, and at Advent Conspiracy we are placing that value above all else at Christmastime. We continue to be humbled by the stories of generosity. We are awed by the blessings of God on his children. And we are awed by his power on display around the world. What began several years ago was just the beginning. There is indeed more to do.

What if Christmas was no longer about *stuff*? What if, this Christmas, we could spend less, give more, worship fully, and love all? What if we did that all year long?

Then we would raise our glasses high, filled to overflowing with the living water that is Jesus, and worship our God who covers all need. Our lives and houses would be full—not of stuff, but of substance, of divine presence, of life!

What if we vowed to do this together? What if God's conspiracy began to transform people from every tribe, tongue, and nation? This is our invitation. This is our prayer.

To the glory of our God—Loving Father, Incarnate Son, Holy Spirit—Christmas can still change the world.

THE
CONTINUING
ADVENTURE

Over this past decade we have indeed been blessed to see God at work in our churches and around the world. But to suggest that this has always been easy would be telling much less than the whole story. As with any sustained effort, lessons have been learned along the way. Strategies have evolved over the years. Some of the staff who helped us in the early stages have moved on.

But hopefully, at the heart of it all remains a longing to celebrate the birth of our King.

Churches and organizations have wondered aloud if this is a water effort. For some of us it is. But it need not be that for you. All we ask is that you prayerfully consider taking some of that money that was going to presents that would be forgotten by February and give it toward something that will last much, much longer. If you're called to invest in the ministry of say, the International Justice Mission . . . or World Vision . . . or any number of local organizations . . . do it all in the name of our Liberating King.

Please remember, these four tenets are merely the

framework that can push you back into the Scriptures as you consider your family and church traditions. You'll discover there are so many beautiful and fascinatingly different ways this conspiracy can take shape. Once the conversations have begun, listen carefully to the Spirit's leading. And listen to each other. We've been reminded again and again that fresh ideas come from surprising voices—young and old.

For those who have been at this awhile: first of all, thank you. Thank you for taking that risk with us all those years ago to challenge conventional thinking and return to the story that changes everything. Second, don't stop now! In many ways, it will be the next generation of leaders and churches that carries this effort into the future. Help us by inviting new churches, groups, and voices into our conspiracy. And then lastly, don't forget to keep lovingly reminding those in your congregations that we're just getting started.

CREATIVELY REDUNDANT

For many of us this seems to come down to what Thom Rainer once called "creative redundancy."[1] It really is embarrassing how forgetful we become. That's why it is essential to remind your churches and small groups of these basic principles again and again. Never forget how relentlessly the other messages will come every December. We will be told redundantly and very creatively that a stack of presents three feet high around the tree is the only and best way to celebrate. Deep down, many now know this isn't true. But do not underestimate the power of this barrage of marketing.

As leaders and influencers, be prepared to counter such measures each and every Advent season. We have found even the "obvious" points bear repeating. Our continual communication of these four tenets and the effects they have on our lives is helpful to each of us. It's our hope and prayer that you'll find some fresh ideas on our website, but remember, we aren't experts. There is no right or wrong way to participate in Advent Conspiracy—make it your own. Head to AdventConspiracy.org and share your stories and ideas with conspirators from around the world. Together we'll spark each other's creativity for the glory of God.

START (AGAIN) WITH WHY THIS MATTERS

However it translates in your church or group, we've found it extremely helpful to remember the words of author and popular TED talk speaker Simon Sinek: start with the "why."[2] All the time. Every season. Again, particularly for churches that might start assuming this has finally become a significant part of their culture, the temptation will be to jump immediately to "what" you are going to do. "This is such a great and obvious idea; we must do this!" And then we move immediately into "how" it's going to work this particular Advent season—the schedules, the strategies, the worship services or small group activities. Now, all of this is important, of course. But what we continue to discover is the necessity to return to the "why." In your own way with your own words, paint the vision with your team or group or church *one more time*: why this conspiracy matters; why this beautiful story still changes the world; why God will continue to honor our effort to challenge the status quo. After all, this is his story we're telling. If we're going to shake up the conversations that are happening not just in our churches but in the marketplace and the rest of the world, then we must keep communicating why we do what we do.

YOU'RE NOT CRAZY

And then there is this: it is important to remind each other that we are not crazy for dreaming these dreams and inviting our families and friends to a countercultural approach to celebrating Christmas. Many of us have discovered what you probably already knew: the stories are the rocket fuel. Of course, this entire movement is grounded in the very Word of God. We will always come back again and again to the rich and textured story of Advent found in Scripture. And it is the Spirit of God who first nudged some of us. He is also the one now nudging you. And it will only be the Spirit who enables this new-but-ancient way of celebrating to stretch into future generations.

But in a very practical sense, one of the ways we can *"stir up one another to love and good works"*[3] is by telling stories. Stories that remind us God is at work. We are not alone. And we really aren't that crazy for being so countercultural. This is what God might use to ignite new thoughts and hopes and action in each of our communities. So, as we now begin to imagine the next decade or two of this movement, how about some rocket fuel? May these examples stir up your own memories and imaginations of what God has done through the Advent Conspiracy and what might still happen.

THE REST OF A BEAUTIFUL STORY

In the summer of 2017 some of us had the opportunity to return to Liberia. At the beginning of the book you read a description of our joy in learning from afar that access to clean water had been addressed in one region of that war-torn country. But now there was a chance to return to that area and see for ourselves. In fact, the hope was that we'd get to the same village where we'd encountered the shocking indifference to our promise of clean water. Surely now that the promise had been honored, the name of Jesus was in better standing.

Driving into this region we heard stories of another horror this land had recently endured—the frightening and mysterious Ebola virus. The countries of West Africa had endured this long nightmare with varying levels of success. Liberia was no different. But the story we heard was that in those areas where clean water access was accompanied by basic sanitation and hygiene procedures, the death rate was shockingly low. We listened to stories of those who entered these hot zones to operate drilling rigs while wearing hazmat suits. Their courage and faith was met with deep appreciation by those who began to see that this was a part of their answered prayers.

Such awe-inspiring stories made the ride into this area go much quicker than before. Eventually we stopped at our first village and were met with an impromptu parade of people, young and old, leading us into the center of their community. Looking around, it all seemed vaguely familiar, but could this be that exact village? Who could be sure? Things seemed so different now. There was life and laughter, dancing and singing here. But eventually we were led through tall grasses, away from the village, down a hill to what used to be their water source. And sure enough, this "well" sat next to a swamp still full of stagnant, gray-green water. This was the village where others had made empty promises in the name of Jesus.

So much seemed the same at this spot. And yet, back in the village everything seemed different. We learned the previous chief had since died, but his successor seemed intent on telling us what a miracle had taken place in his village. We must celebrate in every way possible!

And why not? These elders were no longer resigned to burying their children because of waterborne diseases seemingly out of their control. All you had to do was stop and listen to the giggling and game-playing happening everywhere. This community was teeming with the life of little ones again. God be praised for this.

Oh, and he *was* being praised. For the biggest addition to this village since our last visit over a decade ago was the building of a church big enough for even those in the outlying areas to attend. As it turns out, that parade wasn't just leading us to the center of their community but to a worship service at the church.

This time we listened to stories not of death but life. The elders spoke. Preachers preached. A choir sang. Old people cried. Young people listened. Children fidgeted and danced in the aisles. And the beautiful worship of our great and gracious God filled that airy room. To think this all began when God called a few churches to celebrate the Advent of his Son in a different way. May we even now—years later—conspire together. May God continue to remind us all that he is not finished with us or this world. May we soon be shocked again by the work of his mighty hand.

For you see, the message of Jesus can still change the world.

STORIES FROM CO-CONSPIRATORS

We are a small, 250-person church in Texas. We started doing AC in 2009 because we deeply connected with the heart and purpose. Over the past nine years, it has become the *single most life-changing program* in our church family. . . . The only thing we do is ask first-time participants to project how much they would normally spend on Christmas (gifts, wrapping paper, travel, parties, etc.) and challenge them with the idea that they could have an equally great Christmas with half the amount . . . and then give the other half to AC. Our AC collections have averaged between $25,000–$30,000 throughout. Not bad for a little renegade urban church!

—*Anonymous Conspirator*

Our community has had an awakening in the past year to the poverty next door. Homelessness relief and homelessness prevention have moved to the forefront of church priorities, and Advent Conspiracy gave us an opportunity to make a significant statement over the holidays . . . $21,000 was raised. We were able to present the check the following Sunday to the designated agencies as well as have our mayor and county supervisor come out and share their gratitude to us as a *faith community leading the way* in caring for our city.

—*Jesse*

This was the first year I have had no Christmas debt. That enabled my family to financially support another struggling family in our neighborhood. We didn't buy "perfect" gifts for each other, but we had less stress this season.

—*Anonymous Conspirator*

We are frontline missionaries connected to thirty small churches in the US. This was our eighth Advent Conspiracy. This December, celebrating the birth of Jesus, we provided relief packages, toys, and blankets to 15,000 refugees from ISIS in northern Iraq;

hosted Christmas celebrations at three orphan sites with 1,300-plus children in East Africa; purchased a new van for a Christian Maasai school in northern Tanzania; built a new classroom for an orphan school in Kenya; built a house for a widow and her children in northern Iraq; and purchased medical supplies for the rural clinic we had built in Tanzania as part of last year's AC. *Christmas can still change the world!*

—*Jerry*

As I spoke through the four themes of Advent Conspiracy in my sermons, I was struck by a thought as I was writing my message one day. It struck me that because of our participation and "sacrifices," children that were going to die in 2009 from waterborne illnesses were going to live and get healthy, and parents who were going to mourn the loss of their children would not have to endure that awful fate. They instead would celebrate the presence of clean water in their community, hopefully wonder what motivated people in America to provide it for them, and find that *the answer was Jesus.* We are a church of 175 . . . and collected over $13,000 this year toward the Advent Conspiracy.

—*Bob*

I am Catholic and my faith tradition emphasizes Advent as a "mini-Lent"—a time to consider how prepared we are for the coming of God in our lives and world, with additional time for praying, repenting, and almsgiving. I'm encouraged knowing there are other Christians working to redirect the focus of what Advent ought to be: a time of *preparation for Immanuel.*

—*Anonymous Conspirator*

It has been such a joy to share Advent Conspiracy with my in-laws. Their local church hasn't joined the movement, so they first heard about AC through my husband. Together we are starting *new Christmas traditions* and demonstrating what it looks like to worship fully, spend less, give more, and love all.

—*Anonymous Conspirator*

To prepare ourselves for Advent, I had the privilege of teaching the AC class with a dear friend at our church during the month of November. The most immediate idea I had for spending less and giving more was to send out our Christmas letter as an email (as much as possible) rather than spending money on those lovely cards we usually order. This saved the cost of the cards and the cost of postage. Instead, *we made a donation* to Lutheran World Relief with the money we saved.

—*Lura*

Our church follows AC enthusiastically. We engage each year in a local Christmas tree festival. This year as part of "Spend Less/Give More," we knitted our Christmas tree using over six hundred squares in different shades of green. Now we are in process of dismantling the tree and making it into blankets to send to children in Romania. It caused great interest and was featured in a local paper. *A number of other groups plan to copy the idea next year.*

—*Angela*

We had a bunch of Christmas presents purchased for our kids. It was probably about a week before Christmas, and I received a blog article about alternate ideas to spending. One of the ideas was, rather than give presents, to make a memory with your kids and go on a trip. My wife and I took back most of the gifts, and instead took our kids on a trip to an indoor waterpark and hotel. The kids said it was the *"best day ever."*

—*Anonymous Conspirator*

I was blessed this year by giving my daughters activity-based gifts. We got to spend much quality time together making jewelry, putting together puzzles, and making a soda fountain! I was bummed when I found out that one of the gifts I bought for my daughter from a consignment shop was missing some pieces. I contacted the company that made the activity and they offered to send me replacement parts for free! *I feel like this was God's blessing over my effort to spend less and give more!*

—*Aaron*

We baked cookies for our family members and *divided what we usually spent* among the four college-age grandchildren to help with their textbook expenses.

—*Jim*

When my married daughter asked me if we were buying presents for everyone this year, I told her probably not because funds are tight and my husband and I want to focus on quality time. That week, attending church with me, she heard about Advent Conspiracy. I leaned over and winked at my daughter. *The Lord moved in her heart* so much that she is putting together a group of people to take food/hygiene packages to the home-less. . . . The cool thing is we have several nonbelievers joining us for our own little Advent Conspiracy!

—*Anonymous Conspirator*

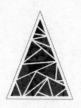

ACKNOWLEDGMENTS

The three of us (Rick, Chris, and Greg) are so grateful for the churches God has allowed us to be a part of over these many years. Without the vision and generosity of Imago Dei, Ecclesia, and The Crossing, Advent Conspiracy would not exist.

What started out as a conversation among friends has now evolved into a global movement. We want to acknowledge and thank the hundreds of churches and families around the world who have committed to celebrating Christmas differently. We couldn't have done it without your creativity, generosity, and support over the last ten years.

To the churches who are hearing about Advent Conspiracy for the first time, join us as we live out the story of Jesus, our Savior come to earth. Together we can make Christmas meaningful (again).

SMALL GROUP GUIDE

SESSION 1: WORSHIP FULLY

(Based on Chapter 3)

"Understand what you're doing and why you're doing it. This is not about anger, disgust, or guilt . . . it is about entering the story of Jesus more deeply with a desire to worship more fully. It is not enough to say no to the way Christmas is celebrated by many; we need to say yes to a different way of celebrating."

1. What was the best Christmas you've ever had? What made it special?

2. In one word, describe what you want to experience this year during Advent? What are some obstacles that might get in the way?

3. What does it mean to "remain in the gospel of Jesus" during the Christmas season?

4. What practical choices do you need to make to ensure that the Christmas season remains a time of focused worship?

5. **Read Luke 2:8–20.** What are some specific ways in which our contemporary celebration of Christmas moves us away from the worship the shepherds experienced?

What can we do to recapture that sense of wonder and gratitude?

The Advent season is our chance to celebrate the wondrous moment when God entered our world to make things right. It is a season of worship. This is the foundation for our conspiracy.

SESSION 2: SPEND LESS

(Based on Chapter 4)

"Spending less does not mean spending nothing. Rather, we strive to thoughtfully evaluate what we support with our spending, and we allow our spending to support products, people, and causes that are worthy of being supported."

1. The authors suggest that the fastest growing religion in the world is consumerism. In what ways do you get caught up in the distraction of "needing more"?

2. Consider all the holiday advertisements you're exposed to. How can you become more aware and less susceptible to messages that say our lives are lacking something?

3. **Read Matthew 6:19–24.** What does it mean to store treasures in heaven?

4. How is spending during the Christmas season a reflection of our heart?

5. What are some ways that you can use Advent Conspiracy as an opportunity to teach your family and friends about contentment?

This is the heart of Advent Conspiracy. More than just an invitation to say no to overspending, it's an invitation to a new way of celebrating Christmas.

SESSION 3: GIVE MORE

(Based on Chapter 5)

"Our giving can actually reflect in some small way the power and beauty of God coming into our world as one of us."

1. What's the most meaningful gift you've ever received? Why did it have a lasting impression?

2. What are some of your favorite Christmas traditions?

3. **Read John 1:1–14.** How does this passage remind you of the miracle of Christmas?

4. **Read Matthew 1:18–23 and Isaiah 7:14.** What are some ways that you long to experience God as "Immanuel" in your own life?

5. As you consider what it means to give relationally, what most excites you? What will be the biggest challenge for you?

All the prophecies, all the promises, came down to one relational gift. The Father gave the most personal gift ever—his Son.

SESSION 4: LOVE ALL

(Based on Chapter 6)

"Advent Conspiracy isn't simply about individuals or single churches giving people a sense of who Jesus is—it's about the entire body of Christ at work in the world."

1. When you hear people talk about addressing global issues such as poverty, disease, hunger, slavery, and education, what's your gut reaction? Overwhelmed? Skeptical? Excited? Apathetic? Why?

2. **Read Luke 2:1–24.** Remember that Jesus was born into poverty. How might this realization change the way you celebrate Christmas?

3. **Read Matthew 25:34–40.** In what ways are acts of service a gift to Jesus?

4. If your family, friends, church, school, or small group were to "love all" this Advent season, what would that look like? What are some practical steps you could take this Christmas season?

5. What are some ways that churches and organizations in your community could partner together in the Advent Conspiracy?

Hopefully by now you're realizing that we believe the Advent of our Savior is the moment on which all our hopes rest. We believe that when we love as we have been so outrageously loved, Christmas can be meaningful and bring change to our world.

For more resources visit AdventConspiracy.org

NOTES

Chapter 2: Idolatry Near the Manger

1. James 5:1–4.
2. Luke 12:15.
3. Numbers 11:18–20.
4. Ralph Winter, "Reconsecration to a Wartime, not a Peacetime, Lifestyle," *Perspectives on the World Christian Movement* (Pasadena, CA: William Carey Library, 1981), 814.

Chapter 3: Worship Fully

1. Luke 1:38.
2. Luke 1:46–55.
3. Mark Labberton, *The Dangerous Act of Worship: Living God's Call to Justice* (Downers Grove, IL: InterVarsity, 2007), 37–38.
4. Romans 12:13.
5. Matthew 1:23; cf. Isaiah 7:14.

Chapter 4: Spend Less

1. Matthew 6:24.
2. 2 Corinthians 8:13–14.
3. 1 Timothy 6:10.
4. 1 Timothy 6:9.
5. 2 Corinthians 9:11.
6. C. S. Lewis, *Mere Christianity* (New York: HarperCollins, 2001), 86.

Chapter 5: Give More

1. John 1:1–3 NIV.
2. John 1:1–3.
3. John 1:14 NIV.
4. Alan Hirsch, *The Forgotten Ways: Reactivating the Missional Church* (Grand Rapids: Brazos, 2006), 131.
5. John 10:30.
6. John 14:9.
7. N. T. Wright, *Simply Christian: Why Christianity Makes Sense* (San Francisco: HarperOne, 2010), 140.
8. Alan Hirsch, in his book *The Forgotten Ways* (p. 131), identifies various dimensions that help us understand the "Incarnation of God in Jesus the Messiah." Though we won't fully discuss them here (or in some cases even use the same terms), we want to acknowledge his and Michael Frost's contribution to our thinking.
9. Matthew 1:23 NIV.
10. Colossians 1:15.
11. Luke 2:11.
12. Philippians 2:7.
13. Hirsch, *Forgotten Ways*, 134.
14. Mark 10:45.

Chapter 6: Love All

1. Scot McKnight, *Embracing Grace: A Gospel for All of Us* (Brewster, MA: Paraclete, 2005), 80–81.
2. Luke 4:18.
3. Luke 4.
4. 2 Corinthians 8:9.
5. Matthew 25:40.
6. Scott A. Bessenecker, *The New Friars: The Emerging Movement Serving the World's Poor* (Downers Grove, IL: InterVarsity, 2006), 59–60.
7. Bessenecker, *New Friars*, 59.
8. Matthew 25:35–36.
9. Reggie McNeal, *Missional Renaissance: Changing the Scorecard for the Church* (San Francisco: Jossey-Bass, 2009), 35.
10. John 17:20–23.

Chapter 7: What If?

1. 2 Corinthians 5:20.
2. Statistics from the World Health Organization.
3. Statistics from UNICEF, 2003.
4. United Nations Fund for Population Activities, *Water: A Critical Resource*, 2002.
5. World Water Council, www.worldwatercouncil.org/index.php?id=23.

The Continuing Adventure

1. Elmer Towns, C. Peter Wagner, and Thom S. Rainer, *The Everychurch Guide to Growth: How Any Plateaued Church Can Grow* (Nashville: Broadman and Holman, 1998).

2. Simon Sinek, *Start with Why: How Great Leaders Inspire Everyone to Take Action* (New York: Portfolio/Penguin, 2009).

3. Hebrews 10:24 ESV.